Roots Grow Backwards

Visions in Midwestern Poetry & Photographs
By the Women of a Naperville, Illinois, Family

Jamie S. Smith • Merle S. Elliott • Claire S. Smith

ISBN-13: 978-0-9793013-0-8
ISBN-10: 0-9793013-0-0

Roots Grow Backwards
Smith, Jamie S. 1951–
Elliott, Merle S. 1978–
Smith, Claire S. 1986–

With other photographic credits by permission as noted.
Editing & cover design by Jamie S. Smith
Layout by Andrew M. Furgal

10 9 8 7 6 5 4 3 2 1

Published by Jamecle Publishing
Printed in the United States of America

Jamecle Publishing
110 S. Sleight Street, Suite k-1
Naperville, IL 60540 USA

Dedications & Acknowledgments

This work is dedicated to all the quiet heroes, especially those who accomplish much because they embrace good over narrow self-interest, and those who have a will to endure and a drive to create so profound they do not give up even in the face of the strongest forces of man or nature. In other words,

This book is dedicated to all Midwesterners everywhere,
whether or not they have ever set foot on this land.

It is also dedicated to the people of Naperville, Illinois, and to North Central College and the Naperville Heritage Society, who illustrate these qualities and remind us how and why they have endured.

The authors and photographer are grateful for the patience and support of their family, especially the 'men-folk': husband/father Neil Smith, son/brother Conor Smith, and son-in-law/husband Brian Elliott. While the gentlemen appear in this book only briefly as guest photographer (Neil), photo subject (Conor), or both (Brian), they influenced nearly all the works.

Table of Contents

The author/photographer is also identified, by initials or name, at the end of each individual poem or photograph. The initials "CKS" refer to Neil (Cornelius) Smith.

*The University of Michigan Hopwood Contest for creative writing requires award winners to indicate in any publication of their winning manuscript that it was granted a prize in the Avery Hopwood and Jule Hopwood Contest for a given year. Accordingly, those poems by Claire Smith included in her 2005 Hopwood award-winning collection are marked with an asterisk above.

About the Poets & Photographer

The poems and photographs in ***Roots Grow Backwards*** are the visions of sisters Merle Sylvester Elliott (photographer) and Claire Sylvester Smith (award-winning poet), both of Naperville, Illinois, and of their mother, Jamie Sylvester Smith (poet/editor), a twenty-plus year resident of Naperville transplanted from the East Coast.

MSE

Trained as a lawyer, but bowing to realities imposed by the passing years, Jamie Smith describes herself as "a marginally competent housewife who writes poetry because I can't not." The insight and simplicity of expression in her poems merge in a voice of compelling clarity; we are moved to examine and often embrace the counter-intuitive. An example: no matter how improbable the growth of a transplant without roots may be, "Midwestern Trilogy" leaves no doubt that roots—or at least roots of belonging in the American Midwest—do indeed grow backwards.

BDE

Merle Elliott, Jamie Smith's older daughter, is a patent attorney practicing with a Chicago law firm. Photography is a sidelight for her, but one she performs with extraordinary vision. Able to see beauty and gauge the emotional impact in a scene at all levels of focus, Ms. Elliott wields artistic flare and technical proficiency to make her visions speak to others, as in the startling photographs—from stark to lush—in the following pages.

MSE

Claire Smith is an honor student at the University of Michigan, Ann Arbor. She has several writing awards to her credit, but her poetry delivers its own validation. Whirling from the unbearably poignant to joyful whimsy, Ms. Smith's poems cross generations of understanding and subject our roots, wherever from, to unwavering scrutiny. The rush of revelation, at least for the self-aware, is not far behind.

About This Book

This book is grounded in serendipity. The photographs were not taken with the intention of illustrating the poems, nor was the poetry written to go with the pictures. Each evolved separately over the course of years until Jamie Smith happened to store them in the same place—and was struck by the links between them. Despite the difference in forms of expression—text versus image—and notwithstanding the independent evolution of each poem and picture, certain themes echoed from verse to photo and back again.

We are all haunted on occasion by a disturbing conviction that something unformulated is important and needs to be defined—brought out into the light and labeled for what it is. Within their scope, the works in ***Roots Grow Backwards*** do just that: offering the relief of understanding and answers—or if not answers, at least better defined questions—from three distinct viewpoints in two different media. We hope some part of this rings true for you.

Tell me how as a child you jumped in the lake.
How the seaweed wrapped around your ankles until
you thought you were going under.

Tell me about braiding each other's hair, about whispering
in notes where the folds were more important than the words.

Tell me the streets were filled with light on Thursdays,
and how when you skinned your knee the scab was worth
the tree.

It's not like a boulder field, where each step makes the journey
back more ominous, it is rows of books in the library
you can't read them all, but they're numbered and ready
to open and smell when you are.

That's the hum from the next room's TV. That means we're
growing quiet. Tell me one more.

Your hands, your fingers, your voice sifting out
the most worn, round stones. Later we can throw them in the lake.

A splash is a splash but the ripples are a story.

CSS

Roots Grow Backwards

MSE

House

You are born to a house
and grow among walls that stop sight and trick
your mind to stopping;
juxtaposed with joists, you cultivate.
And years won't touch your faith
in houses' substantiality

until
you see a house abandoning, with glass gone, in a
field
until you look in the window-holes
from the world on one side and
out the facing window-holes
to the world on the other
and see the gale channeling through
the nothing-between:
a cobweb in space

JSS

Wifesong

Charlie?

There's a dog
in the back,
in the cold;
he's looking to infinity.

Not
much this side of far to stop his
eyes I
guess
on the stiff grass, Charlie,
he's lying—

with his head up
still

Charlie?

I feel how
he feels.

Charlie?

There's a dog
in the back
in the cold,
and a wife.

JSS

MSE

Going Past

My face reflects childish in the right hand window; tinted
oasis, lilac. I begin to look past
the purpley distortion of my nostrils, eyebrows, jawline. Outside this capsule car
the Midwest moseys by.

Land moves: Grain silos draw out
determined towards the cloud cover, grey and gauzed.
Snarls of telephone wires wind
through erector-set thickets of current. Series of scrap metal piles:
hubcaps, wheel wells, hell-bents are sorted
into mounds.

There's an empty tire too large for swinging in
too small to make a fort.
Naked siding, aluminum, bare, silly.
An heirloom grandfather clock that gets slower by the day,
only wound every other week. There are guns growing in the cornfields.
Dreams crusted over with a stale inch of snow. Families
bound in ill-fitting clothes and worse-fitting shoes.

The train rolls through the unending town-land when, on a delicate laced
wraparound porch opening into a frosted field of crushed-once-was-crop

A mother and daughter of four, maybe, bundled tundra-ready, stand
on the top step. That tomato ripe jacket; that tumbleweed of curls; their posture; is all
warmly familiar. They're smiling. They're pointing, holding hands.
I know them.
I've been that hand. I've held that hand.
We wave.

And then, maybe just bit by bit, in upcoming weeks, months, lives,
things start to grow again.

CSS

MSE

When Things Are Windy

We drive cars quickly we steer wheels gently, at times
We both sleep lightly in our bed
But now we're warping east toward Sunday, and
We fought over Virginia
About the Beatles.

You know, the corn plots from a plane
So simple, geometric
Make me remember curved coke bottle picnics and
The different names for 'soda' and how we
Couldn't even get through foam without debating it.

I made a list a while ago and inexorably
You came up not quite six feet
I kept it in my handbag to recall
How sometimes things make sense
At least for a minute.

We made a fort once, safety pins, crocheted sheets
And love seats, It was warm there, pretending we were
Young, that it was long ago but you can't
Make a fort out of airline wool, and we're moving
Forward now, quite quickly.

And there are five hours in the air today
And six emergency
Exits and thirteen tracks
On Sgt. Peppers and I can't help feeling the Beatles
Are easy for most people
To talk about.

CSS

I'mpervious

Itch me, Kid.
Itch me with your bitterness.
Spite out rusted revolution.
Two'll get you ten it'll get you no where:
my tension won't ease your universal acid
and
the only crossed swords
that touch me much
are in my own soul.

JSS

CKS

MSE

Sustenance

Feed a child
twenty-four blackbirds, Excalibur,
and coraled doubloons

serve him
mudpies, and leaf piles,
and willow whips, and whistles, and wishes

love to him

so he'll have fiber to weave
his footprints and shadow
to stand and lean secure upon
later, when alone,
the cold tumbles up from the gorge.

JSS

Perennial

A garden is
hyacinths and lilacs and lilies
all with labels and anecdotes
attached on little white sticks (so you know
where they're from and going).

My mother gardens. She
has time and nice chrome
tools, trimmers and clippers and
choppers and tricksters and
branch breakers.

Gardens are wildflowers from
seed packets, close to dirt and part of it
and teased into a nice rose bush or
some lovely ivy and, wow, the tulips
are blooming well this year.

A garden is the things my mother taught
me, as a girl: mudpies, leafpiles, ropeladders,
the miniature tools she bought me
to dig myself and raise up
my own orchids good.

Gardens are the hours we put in, the
hedges we trim into porch accessories,
Emmanuel we pay to come on Sundays
and water, a fight won against the
weatherman.

I want to kiss the air in a garden with un
censored whimsy and leave without
scientific description or analysis
attached. Maybe get married in one and
kiss a man and have a nice path
out for us so I don't get dirt
on the satin white shoes my mother
will buy for me. *CSS*

MSE

Prodigy

His:
The intellectual brilliance of time's singular
human anachronisms,
and
The eagerness of a kid in a carnival-ride line.

Soon:
Next year, or the next,
He'll leave the swallowed libraries
And enter a room furnished to mate
His aching life's need for creation:
empty

Hey:
He reads sci-fi novelettes on the Burlington Northern
Alternates peanut-butter-and-jelly
sandwiches with bologna-and-pickles
He teases; he mutters

Ask him what it's like.
Being him.

Keep it simple.

So?

Well, the stars are very beautiful
when you can see them through the street lights.

JSS

MSE

Wandering Day

This could be a wandering day: We can join with all the usual places—
destinations whose kaleidoscope of enticements flout all human timetables:

The sandlot:
Grasshoppers congregate, and cockle burrs and milkweed pods ripen
offering clumps of seed-bearing parachutes to air—
and the added delight, as you blow each one,
of planting a weed in some civilized garden.
The empty pods make excellent boats, and cockle burrs are especially satisfying
in someone else's socks.

The meadow:
Field fairies: Moths and monarchs, blue-tailed flies, crickets,
fire ants and yellow jackets, moles and field mice,
and the odd box turtle or snapping turtle offer improvisational theater.
(We'll see with Turtle's eyes the shade whitened base of each grass
stalk, and feel his annoyance at our presence.)

These creatures share billing with tickle grasses, butter-and-eggs,
Queen Anne's lace, and later, goldenrod and asters.
The meadow's hospitality is not to be outdone:
The flavor of tiny strawberries in early summer shames cultivation;
and in midsummer, blackberries at the fringe of the meadow
console the maturing season.

Last, the bramble patch:
The thorn hedge ringing a fairy tale castle is friendlier than this thicket—
you cannot penetrate it; I cannot guess how far it extends.
But it's foreordained you must fight off squirrels transformed to screaming dragons,
and vanquish them with your only weapon—a hacking sword née stick.
Torn clothes and scratched skin will follow,
but the lure of the call to imagined battle is unrefusable.

I turn all these places inside out of my skin and mind—
Come on!

JSS

CKS

Folk Covers

I've got a stack of records in my room.
I leaf through them, all the time, see the pictures on their covers:

Trucks carrying crates
of U-pick peaches, geometric lavender clouds, torn
American flags, psychedelic Cadillacs, southern
Baptist hair, paisley
ties and denim shirts and tulip
gardens, redwoods, dead
couches, boxcars, stages
and fireworks, well-worn shoes.

And every corner just as worn, all
of them bent a little askew, each cover
peeling in splotches, each artist's face
on the front a little dusty
with age, and that smell!
Moth balls, a little sage, oak paper.

I pick them up, look over them, brush them off,
classic rock, blues, Motown, and folk, oh yeah! That
folk. They're all my parents'
records, you know, their music, from when
they were my age, and I bet they
listened to them all the time, in

Bell-bottoms with wooden beads and
cowboy boots and my dad he'd be saying
to my mom, 'you gotta hear this next
one,' and she'd smile, and toss her
bangs as he dropped the needle, and she'd lean
back Indian style and close her eyes and see
all those things,
the flags and cars and hair and gardens.

Someday I'm gonna get a record
player that works, 'cause ours is busted
now, after all these years, and I
think I'd like to have a guy over sometime,

MSE

you know, when I find one who'll get it, and
I'll put on some folk, and I'll
tell him to close his eyes, and lean back, and tell
me what he sees, and maybe, if he gets the
pictures just right, maybe
if he sees the same gardens
I do, I know they did, if he likes the
same songs I do, the ones
they must have been singing, if he'll
humor me, at least, for god sakes, while
I tell him how much I love
my parents' folk, then the two
of us will start a record collection
someday, all our own. *CSS*

Solo in a Minor Key

I knew the song when I heard it last night
It's not
the first time I've heard it;
tune's cranked through a passel of times
just never could
bear to notice
before

Last night I was listening close
or it would've passed me—left me—
in passage again,
not:
wanting
and scattered
and raining, this
song of loneliness:
raw
footsore
and quietly raining JSS

CSS

Above Treeline

You say:
Time out.

I say:
It's spitting distance to the summit.

You say:
Gasp—I can't catch my breath.

I say:
Oh. Stupid comment anyhow. Nobody spits that far. Hey, you can see so far already, ahead and behind; look at the view. Look back…

You say:
Yeah, I can see back. But do I want to?

I: Depends, doesn't it. Depends on the focus…

You: *Mostly, I see people:*
people who played me for
a rookie, or tried—I see
their mouths, spewing
self-interest,
tarted-up with moralisms.

I: Gauze wrap on gargoyles. That was then.
Do you see them now? Standing here?
Did they replicate and beam themselves into our
present? And even if they did, this time, you—

You: *—would see them for what they are.*

Yeah. I would. I think I would.
I can see I don't know which way to go, though.
And you said behind—and ahead…

I am so lost!
How do I know,
how do I go,
get on with it,
walk the straight & narrow,
tally-ho,

MSE

fight the good fight,
fulfill my potential,
follow my dream,
choose wisely,
reach for the stars,
tell right from wrong,
see the light,
find my muse,
be happy,
TakeTheNextStep
for crying out loud!
when, for all we can
see from here,
one path is a Darkened Gate and the next one a Whiteout?

I: Darkened gates can open on barren landscapes or hidden gardens—

CKS

You: ***Mostly, almost always, barren landscapes.***

I: Do you know how—

You: ***You know I don't know a thing about gardening.***

I: Do you know how to learn to plant a garden?

No comment?

And as for the whiteout? glacier or Glory—
doesn't matter.
Don't you know?
There is no dark path for you now;
with what you have become
If you choose a path,
You will light it.

You: ***I'll buy sunglasses.***

I: Tally-ho.

JSS

MSE

MSE

CKS

There is no dark path for you now;
with what you have become
If you choose a path,
You will light it.

New Year's Hawk

A slender sliver of year
Flirts with annihilation
Cling onto it as
The familiar
December's end is sickeningly insecure

Twelve months' memories swarm:

The lacework of tree tops in bud.
Reinterpreting personal worth.

A universe of wildflowers in the flats where
nothing bloomed for decades.
Rites of passage for the children.

A bumper crop of yard rabbits and
a pair of trumpeter swans in duet.
The blur of time through a starved mind.

Jumbled expectations skitter:
A new year demands the momentous.
What qualifies?

A New Year's hawk answers
Carving the sky
Above the wind vane, above the turret, above the porch swing
It mimes:

Choose a new world view;
Strike from an untried vantage point;
Recreate yourself.

JSS

MS.

I Can't Dance

Music is
lure
intoxicant
Music!
visceral temptress
temptress of feet

Dance, feet!
Nope.

Between the imagined choreographic
explosion and enactment is
a chasm of ineptitude

I can't dance. Hell,
sometimes I can hardly walk.

Music…
The tonal eloquence swells
Music…
In my mind's...toes

Dance, feet!
Nope.

I can't dance.

But you can. I've seen you.

Would you mind if,
In my mind,
I dance in your feet?

JSS

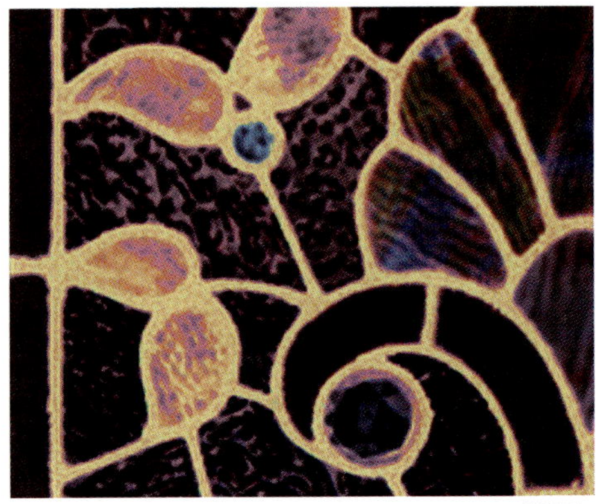

MSE

Arts & crafts

You're nothing like me.
I take the world, its misshapen lumps of polymer clay,
squish it and take chunks and create:
completely abstract bright blues yellows, bougainvilleas,
sometimes brownish and forced, spikes of color fading into each
other, confused
for homes, and my hands will be salt-smelling dirty when I'm done,
and maybe my finished will be half tilted and mangled.
And you? You'll take the clay and get out the instructions and
unfold them carefully
as not to bend the crease. You'll form five small rectangles,
lay them out in a line
with your meticulous black circles for wheels and squares for
windows,
bake 10-15 minutes on 350 degrees Fahrenheit, and Ding from the
oven, I guarantee
it'll come out perfect, from locomotive to caboose, and you won't
care if you do it different or fresh, because no matter, it's good.

I know you're not like me. But I,
instead of eating possibility for breakfast
and painting to-do lists on parking garage walls,
and abandoning speed limits and breaking guitar strings and
expectations
and hearts, and screaming along to lyrics of love songs I can half believe
are true
because you haven't made them not—yet,

I will come down from my paradoxical pedestal.
I'll sit in your basement with you,
hiving from the cat hair on the couch and covering up
with the paint-spattered quilt I always need because it's so darn cold
down there,
letting you talk me in political circles over the president, and tickle me
into ecstatic tangles, and teach me how you do that
card trick everyone's seen before, that still shocks
so brilliantly every time.

Our proximity won't bring similarity, I know, but:
no matter,
sitting there with you is letting me believe;
someday I'll get into law school,
poverty in Malaysia will be reduced,
I'll never get mugged in a black alley behind the dumpsters, under the
hackneyed rusting fire escape, and that maybe, maybe,
after this episode is over,
you'll pause the half-cocky pursuit of
perfection, you'll let me show you
how to come up from the basement,
and tear up the instructions,
and we'll write some out of tune, lyrically
nonsensical love songs of our own.

CSS

Fleeting

He collects clocks. In

his haven just east
of town, just shy of
ancient,
his rambling anachro-house
houses
old chronometers:

On the tilted shelves above the paperbacks,
the straggle
ferns and
the Yellow Pages he's got
the Steeple clock, the Vienna,
the Shelf Library clock (Old),
the Shelf Library (New)
the Parlor clock, Farmer's clock,
the Office clock

And that ain't all
Freestanding, by the front stairs' carved
balustrade
ruminates a ponderosity:
A clock grandfather
Like no other

Its chimes:
Symphonic orchestra at 10:57
Father at 10:58
At 10:59 the securing Earth
But at eleven, humility:

At eleven the massive chimes
                    whisper
          quick, intricate
          like a wren in a redwood.

JSS

MSE

Midwestern Trilogy
I.

I am not native to this place

        but my daughter was born here

I would not choose this place—
so flat it makes not even a gesture
towards embracing those who live here

        but my daughter was born here

I could not stomach the parodies men have
grafted on this landscape
in the name of shelter,
straining to re-embody other places, beautiful places, places
remembered

        except: my daughter was born here

I am not native to this place and
would not choose it
but I find roots grow backwards

JSS

MSE

Midwestern Trilogy
II.

As you travel the summer highways
from the
        East Coast to the West
        or the West Coast to the East
        across this country

You pass through (or by)
        all the small towns of the middle west
        bordered by plat-sized polygons of crops

Pass each community
        with its town square of browning grass and bronze
        statue,
        Its middle-aged houses with
        well-tended gardens, and
        porches baking in the sunshine

And you ask yourself (without actually caring)
"I wonder what the townfolk are like here?"
    Townfolk,
What are you like?

We can tell you:
We harbor among us the same
    fools idiots quitters
    and quiet heroes
as any other enclave of humanity.
No more idyllic and no less noble,

but perhaps
a shade more guided by
enabling moderation
than those who breathe salt air. *JSS*

MSE

Midwestern Trilogy
III.

This is a place of power
The power of nature unmoderated
Where the great green wind
a thousand miles across
tumbles over the plains and on and on
and on

This is a place of power
The power of nature unmoderated
Where the great green wind
alters the landscape from
subtropic to arctic or
arctic to subtropic
in an afternoon

This is a place of power
Where the people draw will
from nature unmoderated
from the great green wind
its cruelty fosters endurance
its wildness drives creativity

Continentally median but no reservoir of
averageness here;
reservoir of strength.

JSS

MSE

Tilted-Spoon

He wears salt-stained
clogs, hole in the left toe, kicking dust babies and candy wrappers
under the pedal of his '94 Bonneville
and I'm learning him exponentially
each time a new track starts on the CD:
just when I'm thinking reggae, maybe, or classic rock,
he shocks me with some sweet bluegrass twangs.

Twenty minutes ago I poked him,
square in the chest, just left of the breast pocket
on his navy button-up, linting. He blushed,
and I laughed. Met just three
hours ago, friend of a friend and it was the first
time we'd ever touched.

He defends every song that
comes on, mostly claims to better like
'their older stuff,' I tell my
funniest stories, the one about the
time in Wisconsin, when I met a waitress, then
crashed the car, came home.

Says his favorite things are
Georgia porches and the
way his feet sink into Tennessee's
red dirt. I tell him I love
sun-faded denim and pool halls.
Really, though, I just like the way that sounds:

Pool Hall.

MSE

So we decide to find all those things,
drive to Tennessee, right now, tonight!
and pluck ourselves a pool hall.
See how charming his soundtrack
sings when it's been on
repeat for four hours, and
his touted ruby dirt is dusting up the back
windshield

Maybe it won't work. Maybe
we'll get lost on 23, or the car will stumble into
a flat tire, or we just won't find
anything worth the trip in Tennessee.
But I think we'll go anyways
'Cause this one time, I went
to Wisconsin with some guy, and
it didn't work out with him, really,
but we did meet this waitress, who
took us out for pancakes at the
Tilted-Spoon diner, and told us how much
she loved her husband, and they
met, as kids, 18, some Friday night
when they didn't expect it, under the yellow
antiqued chandeliers of Kenosha's
one and only Pool Hall. *CSS*

With Her Money, I Buy Myself

Mid-calf boots, one-hundred percent goat skin. Irrationally priced denim in offensive quantities. A mesh scarf that could catch fish. A cloudy-blue blouse, with pompadouring sleeves and ruffles. High-tops sauntering past cool, teetering on ill, sick, *fly.* A houndstooth coat, cashmere cardigans, ironically white pumps.

Mom, I'm going shopping. (I'm hanging on the door frame)

A PETA enraging rabbit fur vest. A fitted cocktail dress worthy of Gatsby.

Again? What, not enough clothes? (teasing from her seat)

A crochet belt. Peacock-feather earrings. Andy Warhol printed T-shirts.

Yes.

A military-patch marsh green sweater. Oversized tees, bearing peeling off iron-on letters.

Can I come? (Awkwardly straightening up. My mother cannot walk without cane, cannot stand without my arm. She shakes when she talks, she spills when she eats, she coughs when she sings. Her laughter hurts. She's hopeful.)

Classically embroidered cowboy boots. Clogs with a shepherd-depicting ribbon across the arch.

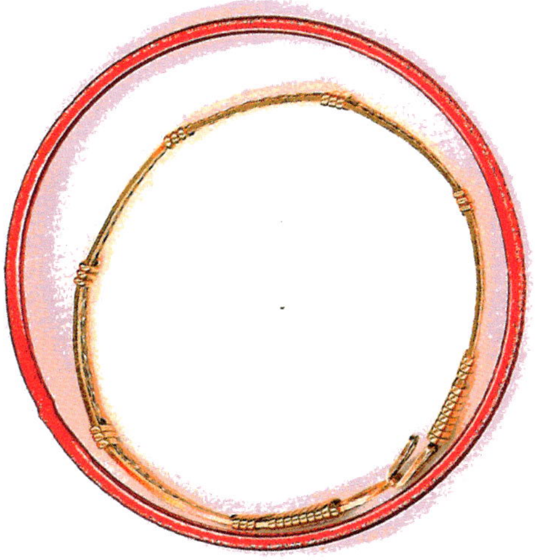

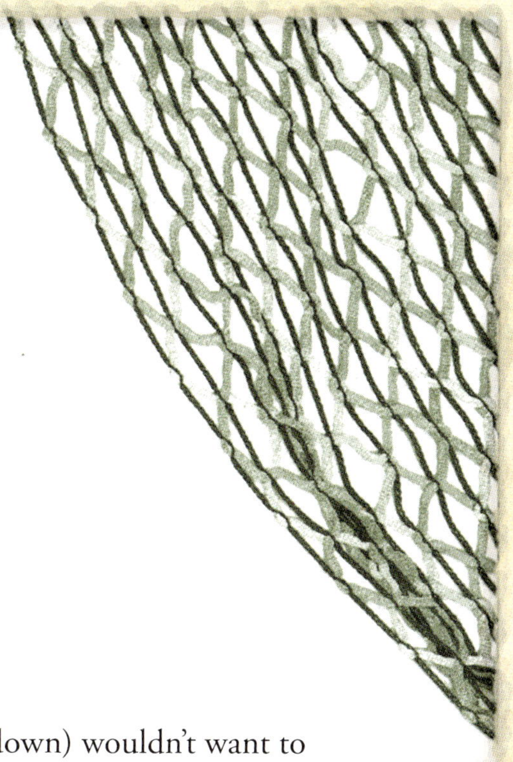

No, I'm just going to be quick, you…(would slow me down) wouldn't want to come.

Bohemianly reminiscent ponchos. Pea coats, down coats, fleece coats, track jackets, house coats.

Are you sure? (Fingering her cane, she fumbles and drops it. My mother bends to pick it up, grateful for the excuse to compose the dejected look on her face.)

A pink-grommeted tote. A sheepskin shoulder bag. A mauve suede clutch.

Yes.

So I shop. By myself.

Mustard colored cords. A cider top that billows from an empire waist. Armloads of lucite bangles. Concert T-shirts from shows I loved, shows I hated, shows I never even went to. Takes 4 tins of 20 pills a day. A brooch faced with Frida Kahlo. The last steps she ran two years ago, from second to third base. Vintage laced corsets, Moroccan beaded tunics. The way her hair flew out behind her. A candy striped skirt with a handkerchief hem. The sole of her left shoe limp-worn down weeks before the right. The stroller she uses for support, too embarrassed to use a walker. Red or blue? Small or medium? Paper or Plastic? Credit or Debit?

CSS

Home

The wind that hoots in the aerial
and mourning doves' altercations on sills
are comforting.
There's a hole in the upstairs floorboards
the size of a foot
but so familiar it never envelops one.
The parquet ripples, the plaster sags;
and a near infinite collection of
corners harbors
dust babies and old desires.

I am
here.

I begin here.

JSS

MSE

My New Car

I'd like a car
for my birthday, honey, one
like you build for the
tattooed men coming in
to your shop.

And if you do
make a car
for me, a hot-rodding,
fuel burning, winged machine,
What color would you use
for the scallops, the flames,
what song
would you hum
while you painted?

Would you make the boys help
you? Light up the welder
all afternoon? Or finish
the paying jobs first, leave
my baby pushed back?

Would you make it
a Ford from '34 to '39?
Would the wheel-well curves
remind you of me, lying
on my side, yawning
as you wrench?

Would you buy
the parts off a friend,
at the flea market,
or drive all the way to Idaho just
for two matching front
doors with the hinges
still intact?

Would you leave a map
in the glove box, so I know
where home is?
Would there be sparks
when I turn
a fast blacktop corner?

Could you upholster it
in leather blacker
than a hearse, add
a chrome-ended shifter,
a double
tail pipe?

How fast would you let me go,
how many hours
would you put in
on the clock, what song
would
you hum
while you
painted?

CSS

MSE

Become

If you can
　　　　soar above the firestorm
　　　　live truly
　　　　wait
If you will
　　　　see people
　　　　inside out
　　　　love them　　anyhow
In time
　　　　you will become
　　　　a woman of power
　　　　a man of joy.

JSS

MSE

S. Mazzarella

MSE

Bimillennial Child

'Bimillennial' child?
All right.

If you say so.

Your confidence,
youth-fueled,
infused with ignorance,
highlights my hesitation.

Not that I won't go, mind you—
Naturally, I want to go—

It's just, I'm connected to my past
profoundly;

Birth roots and death roots:
War stories, family stories, nurtured
slights,
nurtured loves,
plans gone wrong, salvaged (I tell
myself)
by dreams gone well…

And where are we going?
Did you think about that?

Let's go! You say.

All right…All right!
We'll…
sing, chant, howl, roar!
Into the greatest beyond

JSS

Mixed Anthology

I.

Early on, the sapling grew two leaders at a narrow Y
not the strongest conformation, but not rare among mature trees
Over time, the split trunk held, but other weak branches snapped in the storms
We are all of us wounded

The tree grew tall in comparison to the landscape,
its height an attractant to the lightning that galvanized and scarred it
with channels erupted from the bark of each leader like biological lava flows
Wounded and incomplete

CKS

It survived nonetheless, and each year dropped
thousands of seeds into the surrounding earth
Hundreds took hold temporarily, a few permanently
We are branded by the past

The branches supported a wealth of other life
Starlings and creeper vines, chickadees, woodpeckers, insects and squirrels
Now and then the odd crow chased off by the cardinals
Laced with visions of the future

On the mature tree, the bark has thickened and rippled
The lightning scars are camouflaged and immaterial to the tree's life processes
Soldiering on, longing, yearning—

II.

Her childhood home squatted
at the butt of a gravel road
With no family car to drive her from school,
She was mortified at the teacher's offer of a ride,
Sick he might see the unpaved street
Lied to him about where she lived
Then walked home after his car pulled away
She is a corporate executive now
With all the trappings of wealth
Stockpiles symbols of status to pave
the redneck road of her memories
But she knows her need
And that keeps her this side of crazy

Early on, the sapling grew two leaders at a narrow Y
not the strongest conformation, but not rare among mature trees
We are all of us wounded

III.

Another is a brilliant analyst, hypnotic speaker
Yet wives have come and gone
And every ultimate challenge sidestepped
He could talk you tongue-tied but will not try
Agonized over his mother's passing
Mother not his mother
He is adopted
Logically irrelevant,
but to him a flaw in foundation
He has never felt whole

Over time, the split trunk held, but other weak branches snapped in the storms
Wounded and incomplete

IV.

The good wife
The loving mother
The gracious hostess
The loyal friend
The dead brother
Why did she deny his desperation?
Why didn't she insist, before it was too late,
Insist against her nature
That someone intervene?
How forgive herself—

The tree grew tall in comparison to the landscape,
its height an attractant to the lightning that galvanized and scarred it
with channels erupted from the bark of each leader like biological lava flows
We are branded by the past

V.

Yet another loved flowers and fabrics and the
Husband who died when their son was only two
Stranded jobless in the frayed underside of the city
She made do as a seamstress
And cared for the child well enough
He grew in understanding and capability
To the personal strength supporting success and six
Children, grandchildren for her

It survived nonetheless, and each year dropped
thousands of seeds into the surrounding earth
Hundreds took hold temporarily, a few permanently
Laced with visions of the future

VI.

He seeks power and the respect of his peers
All his energies focused on honing the tools
for this endeavor
Energy exploding just shy of
seductive abandon
He effects leadership by mere presence;
just being near him, you want to follow
His 'family,' huge, fluid, is forged by
his daily favor
The gregarious man of business
He evokes both admiration and fear
in his staff

CKS

The branches supported a wealth of other life
Starlings and creeper vines, chickadees, woodpeckers, insects and squirrels
Now and then the odd crow chased off by the cardinals

Soldiering on, longing, yearning—

VII.

We are all of us wounded
She binds the wound of childhood shame with self-knowledge
Wounded and incomplete
Flawed foundation notwithstanding, he abides
We are branded by the past
She salvaged love enough to nourish husband and children
Laced with visions of the future
Prolific grandchildren progeny of a ghost great-grandfather
Soldiering on, longing, yearning—
His drive the energy that feeds those around him

On the mature tree, the bark has thickened and rippled
The lightning scars are camouflaged and immaterial to the tree's life processes

VIII.

MSE

We are all of us wounded
Wounded and incomplete
We are branded by the past
Laced with visions of the future
Soldiering on, longing, yearning—

The tree grows

toward the light

JSS

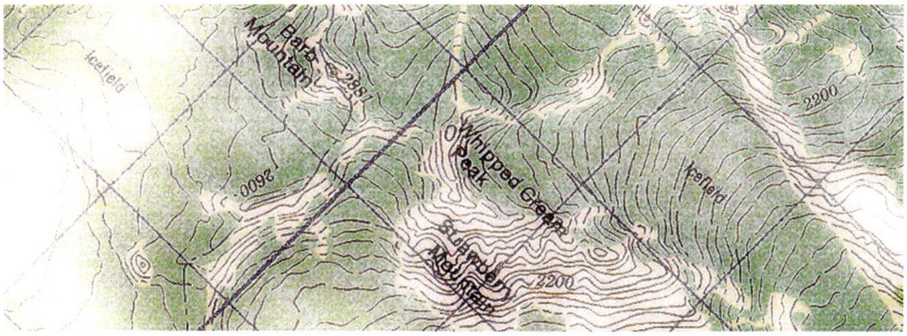

Maps

Last night I was sick, and waiting for you, afraid to fall asleep alone. I climbed into bed and took out a map. I looked at the states, countries: Nevada government land, slot machines, angles. Switzerland winding trains, red-fringed scarves, avalanches. I remembered Colorado, the creek I once lived on, India, topiaries with my mother. It took my headache away.

I imagined all the things I could attach later. I will sleep in an octagonal high-rise beneath a twin comforter in New York. I will take rolls of film in Alaska and forget them in a lupine meadow. I will not be upset to leave them. I will remember.

I will get older. I will take a jet to London for an interview. The rain will not make me sad. I will read lightly on the plane. I will remember being young and become creeksick.

I wondered what you would see: *Mar del Plata,* learning English, one-room apartments, your father leaving, life pro bono. I wondered if I'd ever grow up. I wondered when you'd get here. I wondered if you'd be there to see it. I wondered if you had a map, too.

CSS

MSE

May your roots grow backwards.